Arranging Things

A Rhetoric of Object Placement

Leonard Koren
(Paintings by Nathalie Du Pasquier)

Stone Bridge Press
Berkeley, California

Published by Stone Bridge Press, PO Box 8208, Berkeley, CA 94707

Art direction and design by the author: leonardkoren.com

Printed in Canada

ISBN 1-880656-82-5

CONTENTS

A few words about the paintings in this book

The paintings in this book are not "still life paintings." Rather, they are illustrations of arrangements of objects.[1] This distinction may not now seem significant, but it will be explained later.[2]

The paintings are, for the most part, loosely based on miscellaneous arrangements I, the author, have seen in Europe and North America in shop windows, in store displays, studios, and offices, and in people's homes. The overriding design considerations of the particular arrangements were abstracted and then presented to the book's illustrator in a few words of brief description. Not unexpectedly, some of the resulting illustrations have obvious communicational limitations. Important nuances of arrangement—precise representation of size, shape, and spacing between objects; specific qualities of surface and lighting; accurate perspective—either are not fully rendered, or are rendered somewhat expressionistically (as opposed to "realistically"). However, there is always something "wrong" with the communication of visual information, even in optimal circumstances. In the "real world," for example, gaps in illumination, awkward viewing angles, not enough time to look, and even the viewer's delusional mindset are some of the factors that may detract from an idealized "purity of perception." Additionally, in any depiction of the real world, arrangements are removed from the context of a specific place and transported to "virtual pictorial space." With all that said, I am confident that the illustrations in this book contain enough reliable information to allow the reader to follow the points offered in the text.[3]

The objects depicted in the illustrations—often vaguely generic, sometimes idiosyncratic—are from the painter's collection of things regularly used as models for her paintings. They are mainly common domestic objects found in Italy, where the artist lives. In many cases, the objects used in a particular arrangement appear to be arbitrarily chosen. That is, if the object is a bottle rather than a book, it doesn't seem to make much difference to the overall meaning of the arrangement. The objects are like nonsense words in a hypothetical English sentence;

the words (objects) are gibberish, yet you can discern the meaning from the grammatical structure (i.e., the arrangement of things).

Some final comments: The arrangements represented in the paintings are not necessarily intended to be "beautiful," or even "effective"; they are, simply, examples used as the basis of discussions about the rhetorical arrangement principles elaborated on in this book. The paintings were commissioned and made without knowledge of these principles. I never explained this aspect of the book to the painter because, frankly, the rhetorical scheme was conceived relatively late in the bookmaking process.[4]

What is "arranging things"?

"Arranging things"—the placement of objects in three-dimensional composition—is one small corner of the design universe. Arranging things has two aspects: (1) the selection of objects—*things*—and (2) the manner in which the objects are arranged.[5]

Arranging things can occur virtually anywhere, in public or private space, but should not be confused with arrangements of things that are meant to be works of art. Most arrangements are little noticed, yet some stop you in your tracks. A "successful" arrangement, that is, an effective arrangement, is one that powerfully engages your attention and sustains your interest. What makes an arrangement effective? This book contends that it is the arrangement's "rhetorical power," or finesse, but more on that later.

In the commercial realm, arranging things is omnipresent and goes by many names. The arrangement of flowers is called floral design. The arrangement of objects for photo shootings is called styling. The arrangement of objects in homes and offices is called interior decorating. The arrangement of objects in store windows and in-store displays is called visual merchandising.[6]

Arranging things in both the commercial and non-commercial realms have this in common: arrangements always communicate something. In other words, an arrangement of things is not just an aesthetic expression; it is a communicational act.[7] In many cases arrangement is language-like. A vase full of red roses next to a candelabra and a bottle of chilling champagne "says" romance. Though the domain of arranging things is not nearly systematic enough to qualify as a bona fide language, it is systematic to a degree.[8] A more apt term would be "visual communication system," i.e., communication by visual means. The clothes people wear, hair styles, automobile preferences, hand gestures, and so on—each is a distinct visual communication system. Communication systems, like natural languages, grow and develop through perpetual use and experimentation. In the process, the communication possibilities are extended.

Arranging things in the "real world" versus arranging things in the "art world"

Looking back two thousand years or so to ancient Rome, we can see that the communication system of arranging things already extended to the realm of artistic pictorial representation, that is, what we regard today as works of art.[9] From the very beginning, the things pictured in these artistic representations not only looked like their real-life counterparts, they also meant pretty much the same things.[10] Even 1,500 years later, in the 16th century, a strikingly rendered basket of fruit painted by Caravaggio, for example, had the same meaning, more or less, as the real world basket of fruit used as its model.[11] Similarly, the symbolism of the so-called *Vanitas* ("vanity") paintings of the 17th century was very similar to the symbolism of the real-world arrangements they were modeled on. Every viewer knew that expensive food, alcoholic beverages, tobacco, and musical instruments in a painting were allusions to "sensual indulgence." Every viewer also knew that bags of money and documents like property deeds were symbolic shorthands for "power and wealth," and that wilted flowers and rotting fruit were metaphors for "the deterioration of once living things."[12]

By the 20th century, however, a schism had developed between the real world and the world as portrayed in artistic representations. Because of overriding stylistic, pictorial, and intellectual concerns particular to the art world, the meanings of arrangements depicted in paintings and other works of art became different from those of the real world. For example, in a typical Impressionist painting, say Pierre Bonnard's *The Coffee Mill*, the representation of objects in the painting veers away from the recognizably three-dimensional into two-dimensional patterned abstraction.[13] The individual objects in such paintings are visually abstracted to a point where their real-world meanings become indecipherable—and irrelevant. The paintings as artistic entities retain their communicational integrity—if viewed through the perspective of art-world concerns. But the arrangements depicted in the paintings no longer correlate with the real world in an interpretatively predictable way.

IL PATTO COL SERPENTE
A. KERTEZ
SEAMUS HEANEY
FSG

DARIO
VILLA
TUTTE
LE
1994
30

One hundred years later, this divergence between the real world and the art world continues unabated. Today's contemporary avant garde art intentionally functions as an incubator of expanded meanings, conceptual dislocations, and perceptual disorientations.[14] In other words, the real world seems to stop at the museum or gallery entrance. The real world of arranging and the art world of arranging—which now includes "installations" and sculptures that look like arrangements, in addition to still life painting—manifestly occupy separate conceptual domains.[15] (In this book we are concerned only with arranging things in the real world, where the visual communication system is relatively transparent to everyone, not just the cognoscenti.)

Why a rhetoric of object placement (i.e., arranging things)?

Most arrangers of things work intuitively. They have "feelings" about what objects go where, with what. They "sense" when arrangements "work," or don't. They create in a non-analytical state of mind—which is to say they're largely unaware of what their arrangements mean in intellectual terms.[16] The domain of arranging things is, beyond a doubt, critically underdeveloped. The ideas and language available to arrangers are meager, and these come mainly from the commercial realm, where deep thinking about meaning has little relevance. Commercial arrangements are intended to be "appealing," "enchanting," and "seductive." These are, in fact, the kind of terms used liberally in visual merchandising texts.[17]

To me at least, this language of visual merchandising is flaccid and limited. So is the customary language of design and art education: "unity," "balance," "harmony," "compositional line, "good proportions. . . ." Presumably these words and phrases are useful to some, yet for me they fail to convincingly identify principles operating within effective arrangements.

Motivated by this dissatisfaction, I searched for another way to more constructively describe the mechanisms of arrangement.[18] In the midst of my rumination, while watching the evening TV news, the word "rhetoric" popped into my head. Politicians justifying legislative actions, advertisers pitching products, newscasters selling believability—*this is all rhetoric*, I thought. And then it dawned on me: all communication is rhetorical to a large degree.[19] If you're not attempting to get someone to see, feel, think, or act in a particular manner, why bother communicating at all? Rhetoric, as Aristotle wrote, is "the faculty of observing in any given case the available means of persuasion."[20] Alternatively stated, rhetoric is persuasion through communication.[21] Whether it's trying to convince others that something is more true, more virtuous, or more desirable—all communication is rhetoric in action. And if arranging things is a form of communication, which this book contends it is, then why not look to rhetoric as a means of identifying its principles?

A mini-history of rhetoric

According to historical accounts and legend, rhetoric in the Western world was first codified in ancient Greece 2,500 years ago.[22] Tyrannical oligarchies were overthrown in Greek colonies on Sicily, notably Syracuse, and in Athens. Citizens who had lost their land during the dictatorships could appeal to the assemblies established by the new democratic governments. In the Greek legal system of this time, both parties in disputes had to personally present their cases—there were no lawyers. Korax, an enterprising Syracusan familiar with disputation, began teaching his fellow citizens, for a fee, systematic means of arguing their cases persuasively. A student of Korax brought his system of rhetoric—a kind of superior common sense embellished with stylistic devices—to Athens, where it was subsequently taught by a group of itinerant teachers called Sophists ("wise ones").[23] After initially repudiating rhetoric because of its intrinsic amorality—rhetorical skills alone could make the ostensibly less virtuous argument/case triumph over the more virtuous one—its usefulness in responsible democratic civic life, in discussions and debates, was widely accepted in Greece by the 3rd century B.C.E.[24] Later, rhetorical training became an important part of political life and higher education in the Roman Empire.

In subsequent centuries, the Christians, who were leery of ideas developed and used by the pagan Greeks and Romans, embraced the study and practice of rhetoric. Saint Augustine was a rhetoric teacher before his conversion to Christianity in 386. He contended that rhetoric could be useful in the proselytizing and teaching of Christian doctrine. Eventually, the rhetorical works of Aristotle and Cicero formed the basis for education in Medieval and Renaissance times. Rhetoric, along with grammar and logic, became part of the trivium ("the three ways") that formed the fundamental education for those seeking entry into the clergy and fields of higher learning. The trivium, in turn, was the foundation for the quadrivium ("the four ways")—arithmetic, geometry, astronomy, and music. The trivium together with the quadrivium became what we know today as the "liberal arts."

As Western culture shifted definitively from an oral tradition to that of the written word, rhetoric came to be embedded more and more in the study of written composition and literature, including, eventually, literary analysis and criticism. In the 20th century, in response to wartime needs, propaganda, an offspring of rhetoric, became a field of serious study. Advertising, modern political campaigns, and mass communications in general are also heirs to the classical traditions of rhetoric.[25] In fact, *anyone* who communicates today is profoundly influenced by rhetoric. As communicators we incessantly make choices regarding which words, phrases, images, and/or music to use based on rhetorical considerations—albeit not always consciously.[26] The concepts of classical rhetoric are deeply ingrained in all of our Western modes of communication, arranging things included.

Constructing a rhetoric

A "rhetoric" is a codified system of rhetorical principles, devices, or techniques. The purpose of any rhetoric is to make the dynamics of a specific communication medium more clear, conscious, and rational. Rhetorics (rhetorical schemes) are used as a means of analyzing communications, and as the basis for developing rhetorical strategies. Classical rhetoric, as developed by the ancient Greeks, was originally designed for the medium of public speaking. It was composed of five parts:

(1) *Invention*—identifying and developing your logic and arguments.

(2) *Arrangement*—figuring out how to organize your arguments into the most effective order.

(3) *Style*—putting your arguments into actual language (choice of words, sentence construction, and so on).

(4) *Memory*—creating mnemonic devices to help you memorize your speech.

(5) *Delivery*—using tone of voice, phrasing, facial expressions, etc., to convey emphasis and rhythm.

Since rhetoric was not originally intended for visual communications, adapting it to arranging things requires major reconceptualizing.[27] Following are a few of the immediate considerations and challenges that become apparent when constructing a rhetoric of arrangement, even if only a rudimentary one.

• Words, the basic unit of meaning in spoken and written natural languages, can do many things that physical objects, the basic unit of meaning in arranging things, cannot. Physical objects, for example, cannot represent things that don't exist. The phrase "there was never a bowl on the table" would be very difficult to depict with objects alone. Similarly, "true" or "false" statements like "This rock does not taste like a tomato" would be difficult to express solely with objects. Words can represent abstractions—like the word "abstraction"—that can't be exactly expressed with objects. Additionally, words are very good at condensing immense quantities of materiality into concise descriptions. Try physically representing "a trillion Chinese vases sitting on a billion Persian carpets."

Henri Focillon
Vie des formes
Texte
PUF

Conversely, natural language alone cannot be trusted to accurately represent the actual world. An almost infinite number of words can be used to describe a particular arrangement of objects, and still the essential being-ness of the arrangement will go uncommunicated. Using words to describe real things means a lot of information gets dropped out, and a lot of extraneous information gets added on.[28]

• A rhetoric of arranging things should be systematic enough so you are able to (a) compare and contrast among the same and different arrangements, (b) establish consistent criteria for qualitative judgment, and (c) increase the likelihood that different people, using the same rhetoric, will be able to discuss arrangements in mutually understandable terms. There are, of course, many possible schemes you could use to help you create or understand arrangements systematically. You could, for example, use the I-ching or Tarot cards. But wouldn't a system tailored to the elements of arrangement—specific physical, technical, sensorial, emotional, and metaphoric issues—work best?

• A rhetoric of arranging things probably shouldn't be overly preoccupied with the notion of beauty, however it is defined. Beauty is a rhetorically powerful element for sure, but it is only one of a multitude of important elements.

• A rhetoric of arranging should be easy to use for those most likely to use it. Assuming it is for designers and the like—people generally distrustful of systematic approaches not "natural" to their intuitive way of working—simplicity is paramount. The rhetoric shouldn't be too highly detailed, time consuming, or difficult to use. It should be streamlined, but not so much as to become simplistic and thereby ineffectual.

DOM

Eight rhetorical principles

Below are the eight components—principles—of a provisional rhetoric of arranging. Why provisional? Because it is not meant to be definitive, absolute, or the last word in rhetorics for arranging things. Quite the opposite, it's meant to be the first of many rhetorical schemes that might encourage fresh design thinking.

This prototypical rhetoric is divided, for conceptual convenience, into three parts.

- *Physicality*—first impressions and technical aspects of the arrangement.

- *Abstraction*—associations the arrangement conjures up based on your store of general cultural knowledge and common sense.

- *Integration*—how the various elements of the arrangement work in concert.

ДОБРО ПОЖА
АЛИЮ!

The purport of the individual principles themselves should be fairly clear, or I hope will be when you proceed to the "analytical" section of the book beginning on page 53 and see how the principles apply in actual arranging situations.

PHYSICALITY

1. Hierarchy. Hierarchy means the relative visual impact of objects and auxiliary elements (such as the ground and background). Generally, the more conspicuous an object or element—the closer to the foreground, the more centered, the larger, the brighter, the bolder, or the more particularized—the more important it is in the context of the arrangement.

2. Alignment. Alignment refers to the spatial orientation of the objects relative to each other and to the auxiliary elements. Physical concurrences and relationships such as perpendicularity, parallelism, linearity, symmetry, and so on, are important here. So is the notion of "precision,"

the degree to which surfaces, lines, protrusions, etc. conform—or non-conform—to each other.[29] Alignment also takes into account spatial patterns such as spacing between objects and repetitions of objects (as in stacking, etc.).

3. Sensoriality. Sensoriality is about characteristics of objects and auxiliary elements that appeal directly to the senses and sense-driven emotions. Features like color, texture, pattern, tactility, shape, vividness, and so on are included.

ABSTRACTION

4. Metaphor. Metaphor, or "metaphoric process," is about the transference and transformation of meaning. In other words, metaphoric process is at work when the essential meaning of an object or an arrangement—the basic meaning in the dictionary definition sense—gets transferred to, or transformed into, something else. This occurs when *a smooth rock, a conch shell, a bottle of sunscreen lotion,*

and a large towel sitting on a beige surface cease to be merely four objects on the floor but instead are transformed into a symbolic equivalent of "the seashore." Allusion (when one thing refers to another), simile (when one thing is explicitly compared to another), and synecdoche (where a part of some thing stands for the whole thing, or vice versa) are metaphoric processes of this type. In more complex metaphors, two things (or meanings) are compared, and in the process a third thing (or meaning) is created. For example, *a pair of glasses* (thing #1) *sitting on top of a book* (thing #2) suggests either that someone is about to, or has just finished, reading (the created meaning). Metaphors of this type include paradox (two seemingly self-contradictory things that nevertheless seem to be true), irony (when a thing implies its opposite meaning), hyperbole (self-conscious exaggeration), and so on.

5. Mystification.[30] Mystification occurs when aspects of an arrangement don't make sense, but seem like they should: a bottle of plant fertilizer as part of an arrange-

ment of cake ingredients, for example. Sometimes mystification is purposeful, as in intentional ambiguity and mystery. But sometimes mystification is a product of ineptitude, an arranger's unclear thinking resulting in confusion.

6. Narrative. Narrative involves spinning a probable story out of all the information provided by the foregoing rhetorical principles. In other words, figuring out what the arrangement means, *in toto*, after considering hierarchy + alignment + sensoriality + metaphor + mystification. It could be a linear story, an abstract story, or simply the description of a scene.

INTEGRATION

7. Coherence. Coherence refers to the arrangement's intelligibility: how clear the ideas and sensations are and how well they relate to one another. Coherence depends on the arranger's adherence to the conventions and forms that we—as a culture or subculture—implicitly use to

structure our visual communications. An important dimension of coherence is consistency. Consistency can be expressed as "theme" (an overall motif suggested by the arrangement), "rationality" (natural and/or logical connections manifested in ordered sequences, geometry, and other kinds of ostensible reasoning), "homogeneity" (samenesses between elements of the arrangement, like a pervasive color scheme, repetitive shapes, etc.), "clustering" (as when objects are stacked, squashed, or otherwise physically adhere to each other), and so on.

8. Resonance. Resonance is the measure of how long and how deeply an arrangement sustains your interest and the degree to which it "reverberates" in your mind, that is, generates and stimulates new ideas and sensations.

MARMITE

Using the rhetorical principles

The eight rhetorical principles function as the basis of a descriptive language for thinking about and discussing arranging things. Although no explicit attempt will be made here to teach you how to use these principles to create effective arrangements—that is beyond the scope of this book—in the coming pages you will see how these rhetorical principles can be applied to the analysis of arrangements. Through a reverse-engineering perspective, that is, by dissecting arrangements to see how they are put together, you will observe the implications of specific individual design decisions in the making of the whole.

When working on your own arrangements, both in the creation and analysis of them, it may be helpful to go through the principles in order, 1 through 8. Each successive principle is based, to a greater or lesser degree, on all the preceding principles. Likewise, moving back and forth between principles—*not* in order—might also be insightful. You can't possibly note all the rhetorical information embodied in a particular arrangement; it is virtually limitless. But you can try. The more variety, subtlety, and complexity you unearth, the better. Making and seeing are intimately connected, so the more you can "see," the more you can "make."

Another point: The same compositional element—object, object juxtaposition, or ground/background—will have different meanings when viewed through the lens of different principles. "Flatness," for example, can be an aspect of alignment, a quality of sensoriality, a metaphor, or an overriding consideration of coherence or resonance.

At times it may seem that this entire analytical process merely fosters imaginative excess. But since meaning is only in your mind and not inherent in the objects or arrangements themselves, what else can you do but take imaginative, creative leaps into the unknown? This exercise *is* autobiographical; you are describing the way *you* see the world.

Brief rhetorical analyses of the arrangements pictured in this book [31]

Cover

HIERARCHY No one single object visually dominates the others.

ALIGNMENT All the objects are aligned relative to the book: either touching the edge, or sitting on the cover. The book is precisely parallel with the viewing plane.[32] All the other objects line up in two rows, approximately parallel with each other and with the viewing plane.

SENSORIALITY About half of the objects are cool-colored blue or white; the rest are warm-colored brown to beige. In contrast to the hard rectangular shape of the book (and straight edges of the clothespin), all the other objects are soft, curved shapes—roundish or ovoid—with many voids. The shapes of all the objects, however, are distinctly different from one another. All the objects have strong sensual appeal. All the objects are illuminated so that the details are clear and they stand out boldly from the neutral-colored background.

METAPHOR The book functions as a *central meeting place* on and around which all the objects *hang out.*[33] The *eclectically diverse* objects, and the manner of their arrangement, seem very much like those of an *archetypal still life painting.*

NARRATIVE This is an arrangement of dissimilar objects assembled, most likely, as a set-up for a still life painting or photograph.

COHERENCE The blue book is the physical nexus of all the objects. Though quite different in type and function, the objects are consistently sensually compelling. The allusion to traditional still life painting solidifies the aesthetic logic and legibility of the grouping.

RESONANCE The sensorial charge of the individual objects is intensified by their proximity to one another. The still life painting metaphor alerts you to possible art-historical allusions and related symbolic suggestions.

Page 6

HIERARCHY The object on the right has slightly more initial visual impact than the object on the left.

ALIGNMENT The objects are aligned, considering their different shapes and sizes, the same way as much as possible. Both objects—barely touching and parallel to each other—are centered in and parallel with the viewing plane. (The left object has a hard right angle enabling it to more accurately align with the viewing plane.)

SENSORIALITY Both objects have strong but diametrically opposite kinds of sensual appeal. The hard object on the left is a complex shape—both rigid geometric and yielding organic forms together—with a dull metallic finish. The soft object on the right is an irregular ovoid shape with evocative interlocking purple and white variegations. The warm background seems like a mixture of the two objects' colors.

METAPHOR When two distinctly different objects are isolated from everything else and lying side by side like this, *the impulse to compare and contrast* them is almost an automatic reflex. The *anthropomorphic, metallic arm-like appendage* of the left object seems to be giving the right object *a friendly tap on the shoulder*—which implies that the objects are *machine and vegetable buddies*. The *vast differences* between the two objects are emphasized: *natural and manmade, monochromatic and bichromatic, the patterned and the plain, the tactilely hard and the tactilely soft. . . .*

MYSTIFICATION Why are these two objects that have nothing in common but vaguely similar in size, side by side? Is this supposed to be a meditation on objectness, or is something else going on here we can't discern?

NARRATIVE Here are two different and interesting objects we're supposed to look at. Why? We don't know.

COHERENCE The companion alignments and the comparison reflex triggered by these two diametrically different objects are the compelling themes of the arrangement. The background color also serves as a kind of connective tissue. Distracting a bit from the coherence is the absence of any apparent rationale for the choice of these particular objects.

RESONANCE The stark, contrasting sensuality and the subtle suggestion of anthropomorphism provide ample impetus for pondering the "why" of the pairing—at least for a few moments.

Page 9

HIERARCHY All of the objects are perceived pretty much as a mass, at the same time. Subsequently your focus of attention shifts back and forth between the individual objects.

ALIGNMENT The objects are precisely centered along an invisible vertical axis that is precisely perpendicular to the horizon and parallel with the viewing plane. The top two objects are side by side on the same plane.

SENSORIALITY All of the objects are simple, basic shapes. The two objects at the bottom of the arrangement feel dense and heavy; the two objects at the top feel light and airy by contrast. The bottom objects have rich, warm colors; the top objects are transparent and cool. All the objects seem surreally vibrant, positioned as they are against the particular light hues of the warm ground and the cool background. The horizon line between the ground and background is dark and fuzzy.

METAPHOR The two glasses side by side seem to *beg comparison.* The darkening at the horizon looks like *a stormy sky meeting the earth.* The wood block dividing the glasses above from the flower pot below looks like *a division line in a fractional notation*, or a *balance beam* of some sort. The wood block and pot, together, function as *a pedestal* for the glasses. There is an almost *emphatic sense* of *reason and rationality* to the object arrangement.

MYSTIFICATION The pictorial intensity of this group of blatantly plain, nondescript objects seems misplaced. The metaphoric suggestions seem reasonable, but the objects somehow *unworthy*. Is the arrangement supposed to be absurd, or what?

NARRATIVE This is more than an arrangement; this is a grand, epic "event" occurring in existential space and having to do, most likely, with the enigmatic relationship between two glasses.

COHERENCE The clear rationality suggested by the precise object alignments, the strong and vivid sensoriality, and the suggestion of comparison all together offer many strands of connectiveness. This cohesion, however, is undermined slightly by doubts about the merit and meaning of the objects themselves.

RESONANCE Each object, and the setting, have outsized sensorial effect. This is enough to sustain interest in the arrangement until you run up against the conceptual deadend.

Page 10

HIERARCHY All objects are of similar visual interest, though the napkin—set apart from the rest—may attract a little more attention.

ALIGNMENT The objects are almost precisely arranged in two horizontal rows, parallel with each other and the viewing plane. The napkin in the back row is centered behind the plate in the front row. The napkin is asymmetrically folded; the bottom section extends considerably beyond the top. The front row is slightly asymmetrical: two utensils to the right of the plate, one to the left. A small bowl sits in the center of the plate, in the center of arrangement.

SENSORIALITY There is a stark tone and color contrast between the objects and the background. The cloth and the ceramic objects are each different shades of off-white; the napkin is warm, the ceramics are cool. The background, in this context, is a disquieting shade of dark red. All the objects are roundish or have smooth, curved edges—except for the napkin, which is rectangular with hard, right-angled edges. (In other words, the soft-edged shapes are all in the front row and the hard-edged shape is in the back row.) All the objects appear heavy to the touch.

METAPHOR This arrangement looks similar to a *typical Western-culture meal service*. The objects, in combination with the background color, *do not suggest a particularly appetizing meal*. All of the objects look a bit *dull and unrefined*. There is no glass or cup to hold a drink, which seems a tad *inhospitable*. This is an *odd and eccentric table setting*; typically the napkin is placed under the fork, not behind the plate.

NARRATIVE Table settings have rigorous, culturally prescribed rules regarding object type, placement, and alignment. This table was either set by someone ignorant of table-setting conventions, or someone attempting a creative—though not very successful—variation.

COHERENCE The deviation from orthodox place-setting rules, the questionable background color, and the clunkiness of the utensils detract from the otherwise total coherence of this culture set.[34]

RESONANCE The unappealing sensorial qualities, plus the jumbled metaphoric suggestions, mutes the resonance of this arrangement.

Page 12

HIERARCHY The two chairs are the most visually arresting objects, then the table/ pedestal, followed by the bottle and two flanking glasses

ALIGNMENT All the objects are precisely arranged, parallel with the back wall and the viewing plane, in a somewhat pyramidal configuration. Similar objects are repeated, axially symmetric, on both sides of the arrangement's central spine. The highest and most centered objects, the bottle and two flanking glasses, form the top tip of the pyramid.

SENSORIALITY The largest objects are brightly—almost jarringly—colored. The smallest objects are pale whitish or transparent—almost insignificant in comparison. All of the objects have curving, flowing shapes. The floor and the back wall are warm, light, pleasant, neutral colors. The entire arrangement is emotionally uplifting.

METAPHOR The objects are arranged like a *typical cafe table setting for two people*. The furniture looks *Italian avant garde circa 1985–95*. The background appears to be that of *an actual room*. The scale of the table relative to the other objects is *odd* and *strange—mannerist* or *absurd*—perhaps a bit *humorous*. The flamboyant colors of the table and chairs are *exaggerations from the norm*.

MYSTIFICATION The inexplicable mannerism and strangeness seems intentional because it is so consistent. But what, exactly, is the underlying intention of the arrangement?

NARRATIVE These objects are arranged to represent either (a) an "avant-garde cafe," (b) a stage set for a theatrical production, (c) an exhibit in a furniture showroom, or (d) some kind of "art installation."

COHERENCE The succinct, functional relationship of the objects to one another is very clear. Everything makes sense as part of the highly structured cultural set we recognize as "cafe life." The consistent exaggeration of form, size, and color, however, indicates something else is going on that is not at all obvious, therefore adding just a bit of conceptual discord to an otherwise very coherent arrangement.

RESONANCE The sensorially charged distortions of this otherwise recognizable arrangement lend humor or a sense of originality. This is a provocative composition that lingers in your mind, perhaps even more so because of the confusion over meaning.

Page 15

HIERARCHY The ground and background compete for visual attention with the objects. All the objects are perceived initially as one mass. Then the individual objects, and the linear sections of the hanging apparatus, are perceived as separate entities of relatively equal importance.

ALIGNMENT The hanging apparatus—and all its sub-elements—is axially symmetric. Thin metal extensions for hanging things are spaced at equal intervals. The objects hang precisely perpendicular to the ground. The hanging apparatus is aligned exactly parallel with the ground/background horizon line, which is at an angle to the viewing plane.

SENSORIALITY The contrasting ground/background colors are bold and discordant, a little irritating in this arrangement context. The color of the hanging apparatus, by comparison, is somewhat somber and dull; so are most of the colors of the hanging objects. Two of the hanging objects also share the plain, linear shape of the hanging apparatus's structural components. One object, however, is silver—almost dazzling in comparison with the others—

and has a highly articulated, detailed shape.

METAPHOR The hanging apparatus seems like a *rational but authoritarian* solution to arranging dilemmas. It also looks like an artifact from a *bygone era* (it is, in fact, a rack for hanging calligraphy brushes). Two of the three hanging objects almost seem to *merge into the structure* of the hanging apparatus. There is an *Asian motif* to the design of the hanging apparatus and to two of the hanging objects. The ground/background colors seem of a completely *different aesthetic realm* from that of the objects. The metallic corkscrew is of a *different order of function and complexity* from all the other objects of the arrangement; it has an *anthropomorphic suggestion*.

MYSTIFICATION What is a corkscrew doing on a device for hanging ink brushes? Convenience (what convenience)? Humor? Absurdity? And what is the story behind the incongruous background colors?

NARRATIVE This is an ink brush hanging rack that makes arranging brushes a no-brainer. We have no idea why the corkscrew is hanging along with the brushes (one brush is in a case).

COHERENCE The rationality of the hanging apparatus automatically creates coherence. Even objects with no apparent functional relationship to one another coexist (though perhaps not conceptually)—as long as they have a hook-like appendage—in this scheme. The incomprehensible ground/background, however, seriously distracts from the overall thematic consistency of the arrangement. In other words, this arrangement is simultaneously coherent and incoherent, depending on your tolerance for sensorial cacophony.

RESONANCE The precise, inviolably ordered object placement that makes this arrangement so coherent also limits the potential resonance. And when the hanging objects have a nonsensical relationship with one another—the writing brushes and the corkscrew?—plus the annoying ground/background visual noise, the resonance is that of mild confusion. On the other hand, the hanging apparatus itself is arcanely mysterious and capable of generating a bit of resonant nostalgia.

Page 16

HIERARCHY The slippers and the chair are the most visually prominent objects, followed closely by the books and the glass of water.

ALIGNMENT The chair is aligned parallel with the viewing plane and with the side wall. The objects are aligned parallel to the sides of the chair. The slippers are repeated horizontally, and the books are repeated vertically. The glass of water is centered on the back half of the book. Every element of the arrangement looks as precisely aligned as possible under the circumstances. Various linear demarcations in the background (caused by changes in illumination, shadow, and material/surface conditions) are counterpoints—parallel, perpendicular, or tangential—to the alignments of the arrangement elements.

SENSORIALITY All the objects, including the chair and even the black slippers with white polka dots, have a light, pleasant-feeling coloration. The color of the floor is about the same value as that of the chair, but warm instead of cool. The walls are light, fairly neutral tones, both cool and warm.

METAPHOR The objects on the chair are the kinds of things you would want in the bedroom next to your bed; in other words, *the chair is being used as a bed stand.* The chair is colored like a *tropical ocean.* The top book is the color of a *summer sky.* The slippers are colored like *stars in the night sky.* The elegant slippers in excellent condition, and books instead of a TV remote controller, suggest *cultured refinement.* The ground and background look like that of *an actual room.*

NARRATIVE A refined and cultured person has set things out, preparing for bedtime.

COHERENCE A methodical intelligence is apparent from the precise alignment of the chair relative to the rest of the room, the small objects relative to the chair, and the superior quality and condition of the uniformly pleasant objects. With the addition of the obvious bedtime narrative, in a real bedroom, this is a very coherent arrangement.

RESONANCE The coherent framework and the agreeable sensorial qualities amplify the sensation of pleasantness. But the extremely precise alignments—a bit static?—may mitigate the resonant potential for some people.

Page 19

HIERARCHY The arrangement is first perceived as a mass. The objects that subsequently command the most visual attention are the portrait-like image, then the objects above the portrait, followed by the books below.

ALIGNMENT All the objects are aligned—imprecisely—parallel with, and/or perpendicular to, each other. All the objects can be defined as being either “outside of,” “inside of,” “on top of,” or “below” each other. The books at the bottom of the arrangement are roughly aligned with each other on their spine sides, but ragged on the left side. The objects as an aggregation are precisely parallel with the horizon and the viewing plane.

SENSORIALITY There is a pervasive feeling of awkwardness and heaviness—both the objects and their placement. The object colors are drab; so is the dark-gray ground. By comparison, the background, neutral and light, offers some emotional relief, as do the white rectangle and bits of red color toward the center and top of the arrangement.

METAPHOR The arrangement seems *tentative* and a bit *clumsy*.

The objects seem to fall into two conceptual classes: *vehicles of minimal information* (the blocks of wood and the open-faced cabinet) and *vehicles of maximal information* (the portrait, the sculptural figures, and the books). The minimal information objects provide *support and structure* for the maximal information objects. The entire arrangement looks like a *shrine*. In a shrine, what is most special and important is at, or near, the center of the arrangement; therefore the portrait is the *most special object*. Objects of lesser importance radiate outward to *guard and protect* the inner objects; the *clunky objects* protect the special ones.

NARRATIVE This is an ad hoc—probably temporary—personal shrine consisting of someone's favorite, or personally meaningful, objects.

COHERENCE The arrangement clearly conforms to the general structural archetype—cultural set—we recognize as "a shrine." But the imprecision of the shrine construction and the sensorial heaviness of the overall arrangement to some degree undercut the "special-making" transformations that shrines effect.

RESONANCE Because it is a personal shrine—as opposed to a shrine with widely recognizable symbolic objects—the more you know about the shrine's creator, the more resonance there will be. The books, the portrait in the center, the pair of sculpted cats—without a little knowledge of the creator, they are just a group of eclectic objects. They are not fascinating enough in their own right, nor is the overall sensuality of the arrangement compelling enough—quite the contrary—to sustain much interest.

Page 20

HIERARCHY The flower on the left is the most prominent object initially, followed by the top book in the middle pile. Three separate arrangements are then discerned.

ALIGNMENT Three distinct adjacent arrangements, with equal but scant space between them, are aligned parallel to the table's edge and the viewing plane. Two of the arrangements are stacked objects; the other is vertically oriented objects contained in a vase. In the middle arrangement, the top book is oriented precisely perpendicular to the books beneath. On top of the top book are two rocks aligned toward the front, parallel to the table edge; one rock is perpendicular to the stack beneath, the other diagonal. With one notable exception—the top book—neither the arrangements themselves nor their component objects are aligned in a rigidly precise manner.

SENSORIALITY The object colors are for the most part joyful and uplifting. The object shapes are simple and basic; so are the materials—paper, pottery, glass, water, and vegetation. The textured brownish table top has an earthy feeling.

METAPHOR All three separate arrangements—plant materials in a vase, stacked books, and stacked mismatched cups and saucer—are *common arrangement sets*, perhaps even *clichéd arrangements*. The manner in which the three component arrangements are all aligned to the straight edge of the table conveys a sense of *rational order*. The *beautiful rocks* atop the stacked books are *non-functional aesthetic objects*. The books seem to be of the *dense, cerebrally engaging* sort. The top book, front and center and precisely aligned, seems *particularly important*. The sub-arrangements deal respectively, from left to right, with *nature, mind, and body* (the refreshment of). The color and texture of the table is like that of *earthy soil*. The cups and saucer are obviously *not a formal set*. The loose alignment of the objects in all the arrangements gives a sense of *casualness*, although the arrangements look *conscientiously composed*—as if objects lying around were gathered *to tidy up the room*. Altogether the arrangement is consistent with the norms of "*good taste*" as propagated by interior design and shelter magazines geared to a somewhat cultured readership.

NARRATIVE A table top in a cultured and artistic living environment (or, an environment aspiring to such). The arrangement is probably the byproduct of tidying up the room.

COHERENCE All three arrangements are individually, and together, logically consistent and easy to read—coherent—because we have seen them, in similar iterations, many times before.

RESONANCE As an ensemble, the arrangements conjure up and propel you into a coherent socio-cultural universe. But after you take in the objects, resonance may be limited by your overfamiliarity with this sensibility.

Page 22

HIERARCHY The objects contained are of more visual interest than the container. The background color is almost as visually engaging as the objects themselves.

ALIGNMENT The container is centered toward the front of the viewing plane. The contained objects are constrained by the shape and size of the container opening. All of the objects are vertically oriented and, except for one on the diagonal, approximately perpendicular to the ground. None of the contained objects is precisely aligned.

SENSORIALITY The background is a vibrant—perhaps even giddy—color. The container's color is a dulled-down version of the background. The coloration of the contained objects contrasts, for the most part, with the background; the colors are applied in a stripe-like manner that accentuates the sleek linearity of the objects. All of the objects, including the container, are shaped to fit the human hand.

METAPHOR The objects outcropping from the *vase-like container* suggest a *flower arrangement* of sorts. The objects look like they are *standing at attention* (except for *one errant soldier*). There is also a *male-female, yin-and-yang relationship* between the container and the objects contained. All of the contained objects are like those *used by designers or other creators*.

NARRATIVE This is an arrangement found on the desktop of a creative professional. It implies "creative work is about to be done here." The position of the objects in the container is provisional, subject to change at any moment.

COHERENCE The container unceremoniously and tidily brings all the objects together; in other words, it literally forces coherence. The unambiguous container/contained dichotomy—couched in *yin-yang* terms—is another aspect of connection among all the arrangement elements. Finally, this arrangement is a recognizable culture set, a standard configuration well-known to office and studio workers. The background color, overly exuberant thus non-professional, detracts from the office/studio allusion.

RESONANCE Though not a particularly interesting arrangement orientationally or metaphorically, it is a familiar one. The lively and stimulating sensual dimensions, however, might, inspire you to muse a moment: "Exactly what kind of work will be done with these tools?"

Page 25

HIERARCHY All the objects are initially perceived as a mass. Then you distinguish the the container from the things contained. Objects inside the front of the container are discernible; objects behind are obscured.

ALIGNMENT The container is precisely centered in the middle of the arrangement. The horizon line between the ground and the background falls midway between the top and bottom of the container. All the objects within the container are vertically oriented and touching each other. One of the contained objects is inserted vertically into another object.

SENSORIALITY The container has curved transparent sides; a round, warm-gray bottom; and a round, warm-white top. A narrow, transparent, tube-like protrusion rings the container just below its top. The container, as a whole, seems sensually cool, hard, and imperviously perfect. The objects contained are all opaque. They are of various shapes, sizes, and decorative patterns and colors—primarily neutral light, medium, and dark tones. The objects vary in surface articulation from the highly detailed to the smooth and plain. The ground is a warm-beige, the background a cool, dark blue-gray; both are rich, pleasing tones. The arrangement's illumination renders everything with an invigorating clarity.

METAPHOR Actually and metaphorically the objects are *bound together*. The jar is the *authoritative* object to which all other objects have to *conform absolutely*. Either the objects are full-size and the jar is *huge*, or the jar is normal size and the objects *miniature*. The light ground and dark background are like *day and night*. The jar is a rather *ordinary type* of the kind we see often in everyday life; the objects are also *everyday and ordinary*. This arrangement could be a *parody of preserved foods in a bottle*. The contained objects have *no apparent functional or conceptual relationship* to one another. They are, in fact, so strikingly different that the juxtaposition is either *ironic or absurd*.

MYSTIFICATION What are the criteria for inclusion in the jar? Possibly a random selection? Or intentional ambiguity? Or an arcane parody?

NARRATIVE This arrangement demonstrates that order and clarity are perfectly compatible with randomness, ambiguity, and/or parody or absurdity.

COHERENCE The arrangement is consistently clear and vivid, easy to read, sensorially pleasing, and absolutely bound together—in other words, extremely coherent. On a conceptual level, however, coherence suffers slightly because it is uncertain what the objects together are supposed to represent.

RESONANCE The heightened sensoriality alone makes the arrangement resonant. The conceptual ambiguity sustains your curiosity because of its uniqueness and originality. But the ordinary and arbitrary character of the objects may ultimately limit the potential for resonance.

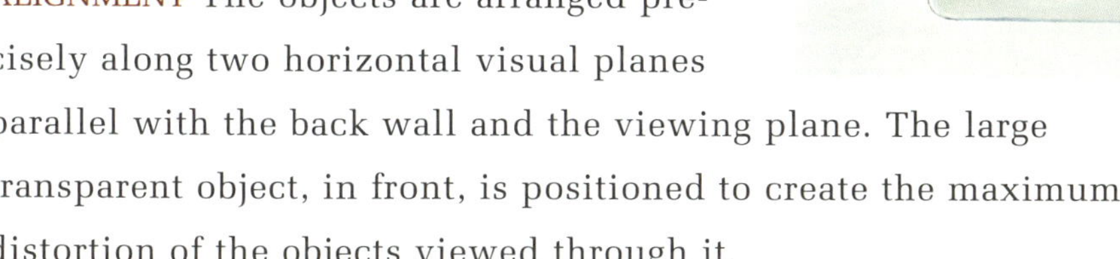

Page 26

HIERARCHY Although different in size, color, and shape, all the objects seem to be of more or less equal visual importance.

ALIGNMENT The objects are arranged precisely along two horizontal visual planes parallel with the back wall and the viewing plane. The large transparent object, in front, is positioned to create the maximum distortion of the objects viewed through it.

SENSORIALITY The colors of the objects, ground, and background are combined and balanced in a sensually pleasing and sophisticated manner. The contrasts between the transparent and opaque, the normal and distorted—and the half-normal and half-distorted—convey another powerful sensual charge. The black, hard edges of the tray offer a strong contrast with all the other soft-edged, light-colored objects.

METAPHOR All of the objects are *containers* of a kind. The precise alignment of the objects suggests a *self-conscious controlling intelligence* responsible for the arrangement. Comparisons are made between *transparency and its opposite, opacity*, as well as between *normalcy and its antithesis, distortion*.

MYSTIFICATION The arrangement is constructed to maximize optical distortion. It is enjoyable to see familiar, ordinary objects in this exaggerated way. The distortion also adds a mystery and begs the question: "Toward what end are these things being distorted?"

NARRATIVE Somebody probably arranged these objects so that the viewer could have a bit of aesthetically tinged sensory fun.

COHERENCE The sensorial qualities are so strong that, together with their associated metaphors, they bind the arrangement together into a very readable expression. There is also a pervasive sense of a controlling intelligence that adds additional coherence.

RESONANCE The distortion immediately and deeply grabs your attention. And then you reflect on the intentionality of it all, which engages you a little longer.

Page 29

HIERARCHY All the objects have approximately the same visual appeal at first glance. At second glance, the tall object in the center and the standalone object on the right are of primary visual interest.

ALIGNMENT The objects are roughly consolidated into three separate vertical groupings. The left objects lean on the (bottom) center object; the right object is set apart slightly from the rest. The overall object massing is upward thrusting and somewhat pyramidal in shape. All of the objects are lined up on the same precise horizontal plane, parallel with the horizon and viewing plane—except for the highest and most central object: it sits off-center on its pedestal, set back from the rest of the objects.

SENSORIALITY The lighting casts all the objects into a moody half-silhouette. The colors of the objects, ground, and background are low key and slightly euphoric—especially the faintly yellowish background. Though simple and familiar, the detailed articulation of each object shape is unusually evocative: kind of sexy.

METAPHOR Each group of objects seems to have vaguely *anthropomorphic theatrical qualities.* The books on the left appear *lan-*

guid. The bottle on the center pedestal looks *noble*. The container on the right seems *complex*. There is even a suggestion of a *dramatic theatrical production* in which each of the three groupings plays a role. Atop the pedestal in the center is an *orator*; the group to the left are *fans of the orator*; the object to the right is a *quiet observer*.

NARRATIVE There is something special, almost charismatic, about these objects set before us so dramatically. And this is very curious because there is nothing intrinsically special about any them.

COHERENCE Silhouetting reduces all the objects to the same chromatic hue and value, and is thus a very cohesive device. The upward-thrusting alignments further reinforces the cohesiveness. Additionally, the detailed outlines of the object shapes, in clear relief against the bright background, highlight the lyrical, quasi-anthropomorphic relationships among the objects. And, as if any more connectivity were needed, the colors of the ground/background and the objects are exceptionally complementary—and the metaphoric possibilities are plentiful.

RESONANCE The same dynamics that make this arrangement coherent also make it resonant.

Page 30

HIERARCHY At first glance you see an undifferentiated pile of stuff. Subsequently you discern individual objects. A longer look and you see that there are actually two piles of similar mass, side by side: an orderly pile on the right and a haphazard one on the left.

ALIGNMENT The objects to the right are stacked—round objects alternating with hard-edged ones—into a pyramidal structure; the objects are either parallel with or perpendicular to the bottom object. The objects to the left are piled precariously and lean on the stack to the right for support. Altogether the objects are aligned not quite parallel with the horizon and the viewing plane.

SENSORIALITY All the objects are jumbled together into an oddly sensuous and intriguing agglomeration. The ground and background colors almost mirror those of the objects. The only deviation from the overall organic shapes, textures, and colors is the yellow and black rectangular object. In spite of the ostensible weightiness of the object mass, the arrangement as a whole feels light and lively beneath the clear, clean illumination.

METAPHOR The stack on the right is *solid, upright, and self-supporting*; the pile on the left *flimsy, haphazard, and dependent.* The color and textures of the objects and ground/background are like those of a *sunny arid landscape.* This is an *eclectic collection* of objects that are all different in type, shape, and function. The three-pronged electrical plug at the top of the pyramidal mass, the highest object in the arrangement, looks like an *antenna pointing skyward.*

MYSTIFICATION A tea cup, a sea shell, a rock, a scrub brush, a block of wood . . . are these objects symbols? If so, for what? And why is one pile structurally dependent on the other? Is this an allegory? There seems to be a sinkhole of unresolved metaphors here.

NARRATIVE This is a strange but attractive assemblage of diverse objects. What it means, we'll never know.

COHERENCE The arrangement coheres because of the sheer physical connectedness of the objects to each other, and the consistently high level of overall sensoriality. There is also a powerful thematic relationship between the left and right piles—dependence and support.

RESONANCE This is an original composition that reveals itself slowly, over a few moments. What appears initially chaotic has, in fact, an overriding structural order. The elusive allegory and metaphors are intriguing, but also frustrating. There is a pleasing balance between sense and nonsense that stimulates prolonged resonance.

Page 32

HIERARCHY The tall objects are initially the most dominant feature of the arrangement. The linearity of the composition is the second most visually compelling aspect.

ALIGNMENT The objects are arranged precisely along an imaginary diagonal line. Tall objects, of almost exactly the same height, repetitively alternate with short objects, of somewhat similar diminutive scale. All the objects are spaced at about equal intervals apart.

SENSORIALITY The tall objects are minimally detailed, vertically oriented shapes. The short objects are more articulated, idiosyncratic squat shapes. Altogether, each object in the arrangement is of a distinctly different type and shape. The tall objects have bright, chromatically saturated colors. The short objects are predominately whitish-beigish. The ground color is a cool tone midway in chromatic value between that of the tall and the short objects. The overall arrangement color scheme is light and cheerful.

METAPHOR The tall-short alternating rhythm suggests a *poetically rational scheme*. The objects seem to be *marching*. What we see might also be *one complete module of a pattern that could conceivably repeat forever*. There is the *possibility of another more complex repeating pattern* emerging wherein every second tall object has a small, round, cap.

NARRATIVE This is a lyrical and disciplined arrangement of common objects that are related by nothing more than their relative physical mass and height.

COHERENCE The repetitive rhythm is the unequivocal theme that makes the arrangement cohere. Though the objects lack a profound relationship of ideas, the pronounced clarity of the composition—in concert with a consistent sensual energy—makes this arrangement highly coherent.

RESONANCE The balance between the rationality of the rhythmic orders and the cheerful sensuality create a lively—bouncy—resonance.

Page 35

HIERARCHY Visual attention begins with the large object at the back of the arrangement and continues, clockwise, to the objects in front, which are of approximately equal interest.

ALIGNMENT The three smaller objects in front are arranged, imprecisely, in a line parallel with the viewing plane. The objects are spaced irregularly apart. The large object is set back behind the front row. Together, all four objects roughly describe a triangle (as seen from above). The three largest objects form the corners of the triangle. The two visible black handles are in parallel and perpendicular alignments with the viewing plane.

SENSORIALITY The faceted, machined-metal objects have a muscular, jewel-like sensuality. The background color has a warm, middle-tone richness.

METAPHOR A *whole object*—an espresso maker—is compared with its *component parts*. The objects have a *robot-like* quality of a *bygone industrial age*; there is also something *toy-like* about them. The background is the *color of coffee*. There is a *puzzle-like* quality about the arrangement as a whole.

NARRATIVE This is what it looks like when you disassemble a simple, old-fashioned-looking, low-tech, espresso-making machine.

COHERENCE The compact and orderly—but not overly fussy—alignment of the homogeneously surfaced objects makes the arrangement easy to read. The fairly obvious narrative is bolstered by the coffee-colored ground.

RESONANCE The objects are arranged in an almost game-like manner—"What do all the pieces have to do with the finished object?" If you are a technology-appreciating espresso drinker, you might be amused. Even if you aren't, the sensual, evocative, individual objects might pique and extend your interest anyway.

Page 36

HIERARCHY Initially the objects are perceived as a mass. The book then draws your attention, followed by each individual object in no particular order.

ALIGNMENT The objects are imprecisely aligned along two parallel rows, parallel with the viewing plane. In the front row, a book is flanked by gloves on the right and left sides. Centered on the right glove is a round saucer with a diameter approximately that of the glove's width. In the back row, a water/oil can's curving proboscis and the curve of a pepper turn inward toward each other. The arrangement as a whole roughly defines a rectilinear configuration. The book is the most centered of all the objects.

SENSORIALITY The warm, red-colored objects contrast—but not starkly—with the cool, muted, off-white ground. The reds, though all rich and intense, seem of slightly different hues. All the objects have sensuous curving shapes, except for the book, which is all hard straight lines. Each object is made of a different material (except for the gloves, which are the same). The arrangement has an energetic, mildly aggressive quality.

METAPHOR There is a kind of *sympathy of forms*, a vaguely *anthropomorphic relationship* between all the curved objects. The title of the book, *Vie des Formes, ironically means "life of forms."* It is also *ironic and playful to assemble all functionally unlike objects* (except for the glove pair) that yet share the same color. Red is a *passionate color.*

MYSTIFICATION What, exactly, is the meaning of these enigmatic objects that are homogeneous in color, heterogeneous in shape and function, and surrounding a book titled *Vie des Formes*? Is this a meditation on materiality and form, a conundrum, or what?

NARRATIVE It's "Red Day" at a hip, trendy hardware store, and this is one of the featured merchandise displays. Another option: this is part of an I.Q. test for children; which object does not belong?

COHERENCE Color homogeneity is a strongly cohesive device. So is homogeneity of sensuous form (with the exception of the book). The intimation of a riddle provides another vigorous connection between the objects, although a more frustrating one.

RESONANCE Both sensually and intellectually, this is a compelling and persistently resonant arrangement.

Page 39

HIERARCHY At first, the front row of cards is slightly more visually engaging than the back row of cups. Subsequently, all of the objects have approximately equal visual value.

ALIGNMENT Two rows of objects are precisely aligned close to, and parallel with, each other and the viewing plane. Every object in the front row is precisely the same size and has a corresponding object directly behind it in the back row. All the objects are spaced, allowing for variations in object size, at approximately equal intervals apart. The repetitive patterns on the front-row objects are aligned precisely parallel with, and perpendicular to, the object rows and viewing plane.

SENSORIALITY The brightness of the objects, particularly the white parts and color bits, pop out of the recessive, deep bluish-gray background. The objects in the front row are all two-dimensionally flat; the objects in the back row are all three-dimensional. The front-row objects feel tightly regimented; each has a different set of symbols and rigidly ordered patterns in either deep red or black. The back-row objects feel more relaxed; each has a different color treatment, pattern, shape, and size.

METAPHOR There are *two obvious, simultaneous progressions*: the face value of the cards increases, one number at a time, from left to right; the cups increase in size from left to right. Both the cards and the cups are *open and exposed*. The arrangement suggests some kind of *syllogistic puzzle*—the ace is to the cup behind it as the deuce is to the cup behind it. The gray background is a *serious color*. The cups are of the kind used for either various kinds of *Asian tea service or sake drinking*.

MYSTIFICATION What is the exact nature of this puzzle? Does the progression indicate ranking? If so, by what criteria? Worst to best? Smallest to largest? Why use playing cards? Is there really a puzzle to be solved, or is ambiguity the intent?

NARRATIVE This is a puzzle that seems to correlate with some intriguingly inscrutable progressive aspect of object connoisseurship.

COHERENCE The arrangement is very clear and well ordered: logical connections, or at least progressions, between objects of the same and different types. There is also a sub-theme of precision alignments. The background color serves to focus concentration. The only thing distracting from this seeming coherence is the absence of any conclusive idea of what it's all about.

RESONANCE The objects seem to pop out from the background, which amplifies the enigmatic, puzzle-like theme of the arrangement. The decorative variety of the cups adds an exotic accent to this otherwise ostensibly hyper-rational scheme. That the arrangement is so tantalizingly simple—keeping meaning just a hair's breadth away—further magnifies the resonance.

Page 40

HIERARCHY The objects are initially perceived as a mass. Then the pencil, centered and high in the arrangement, is a major focal point—particularly the pencil's pointed tip.

ALIGNMENT The objects are stacked crisscrossing, almost precisely perpendicular to one another. Horizontally, the objects are aligned asymmetrically to the left side of the bottom object. The arrangement as a whole is centered and parallel with the viewing plane.

SENSORIALITY All the objects are made of wood: most with the grain exposed; most with hard, crisp, straight edges. All the objects are colored from warm beige to brown. The background is a refreshing, complementary green color, about the same value as the objects (except the pencil). The arrangement has a calm, pleasant feeling about it.

METAPHOR The pencil obscures the letter "n" for "domino[es]," a game in which rectangular pieces are also oriented in a strict perpendicular alignment to one another—a *recursive allusion*. The top object could easily fit into the middle object, and the middle object could fit into the bottom object—another form of *puzzle-like recursion*. The domino box and the whimsical stacking/balancing of objects suggest *fun and games*. The crisscrossing of objects making crosses—as in the *Christian cross*—together with the empty bottom box is a *morbid coffin allusion*. There is a *tentative, precarious quality* to the object stacking. *Dichotomy* is a possible theme here; for example, the arrangement is *balanced vertically and unbalanced horizontally*. The precision alignments create the impression of a *formal arrangement*.

NARRATIVE This is a slightly befuddling, cerebrally playful arrangement about puzzles and games.

COHERENCE The simplicity, along with the homogeneity of alignment schemes and sensoriality, keeps you undistractedly focused on the plentiful metaphoric content. The metaphors revolve around various themes of playfulness. The totality is a persuasively coherent arrangement.

RESONANCE Through there are many formal samenesses in the arrangement, there are also conspicuous differences. This interplay of sameness and difference, plus the many puzzle allusions, keeps this arrangement dynamic and vibrant, i.e., resonant.

Page 42

HIERARCHY The poster is the most visually compelling object, then the red camp stove.

ALIGNMENT The poster is precisely aligned parallel with the horizon line, and centered in the viewing plane. The stove is aligned in front of and off-center and perpendicular to the poster.

SENSORIALITY A lot of visual energy is pumped out of the limited color palette. There are five or six shades of gray—light to dark, cool to warm—and a bright, sensuous red. There is a stark sensorial contrast between the flat gray poster and the full-bodied, three-dimensional red stove. The medium-gray ground has so much presence, it almost seems like a third object.

METAPHOR The man pictured, Mikhael Gorbachev, arguably caused—or permitted—the dismantling of the Soviet Union; he *ignited the ideological edifice* of his country. The gas-filled camp stove is an *incendiary device.* The red control knob—red is the *traditional communist color*—of the stove is roughly positioned where Gorbachev's *Communist Party lapel pin* would go. Gorbachev was a man of *enlightened ideas* and *luminescent personality.* He also was engulfed in the *explosive changes of his own ignition.* Alas, Gorbachev is rendered as a *flat, colorless memory* as opposed to the *lively, colorful reality* of the *real-world stove.* Gorbachev was the last leader of the classical *dull, drab, gray* Communist empire/era. On the other hand, the casualness of this arrangement—hanging the poster with masking tape—suggests something *carefree.* Similarly, the spindly, bent-metal *insect-like/claw-like metal stove flanges* are playful in this context. The arrangement as a whole is a *treasure trove of comparisons and contrasts.*

NARRATIVE This is a paean, both reverential and humorous, to Mikhael Gorbachev.

COHERENCE If you know who the man in the poster is, the arrangement has immense metaphoric coherence on many levels; if you don't know, it has little coherence of any kind.

RESONANCE Though the arrangement has some intrinsic resonance on a purely sensorial level, it really takes off when you know what the objects in this original and engaging composition represent—the silly, the serious, the ironic. . . .

Page 48

HIERARCHY The red object draws your initial attention; next the objects, altogether, are perceived as a mass—with the possible exception of the thin horizontal appendages. There is an impulse to read the label of the object in the center.

ALIGNMENT All the objects are precisely stacked, symmetrically, along an imaginary vertical axis; the stack of objects is precisely parallel with the viewing plane. With the exception of the thin horizontal appendages, all the objects are oriented vertically.

SENSORIALITY The coloration of each object—with the exception of the thin horizontal appendages—is highly saturated: happy colors. The colors in the upper portion of the arrangement are brighter than those in the lower. The background is a soft, grayish green that agreeably contrasts with the colored objects.
With the exception of the dark portions of the thin horizontal appendages, each object has a pronounced round and/or cylindrical shape. All the objects are manmade or crafted except for the natural horizontal appendages. All the object shapes are fairly basic and simple.

METAPHOR The objects are arranged to look like a *humanoid creature*. All the objects are *generic in character* except for the object positioned where the *stomach* goes, a food product *beloved in Great Britain* but *satirized in the rest of the world*. All of the objects are *solid and robust* in contrast to the *spindly horizontal appendages*. All of the objects belong to *different functional categories*. The barbells possibly represent the idea of *strength*. The thin horizontal appendages look as if they might be pieces of tree branches with tumescent flower or leaf buds—*latent vitality*.

NARRATIVE This is a cheerful, light-hearted, spring-season promotion for an imported food product.

COHERENCE To be readily perceived as an obviously anthropomorphic entity—which this arrangement clearly is—the composition must be coherent. The arrangement's festive sensoriality and quirky metaphors reinforce the mood and spirit of the theme.

RESONANCE Anthropomorphism is, by its nature, resonant. The kind of objects used to construct the robot-like entity evoke some good-natured humor and a bit of absurdity. The vivid color combinations enliven and amplify these responses.

Page 51

HIERARCHY Every element of this arrangement is visually compelling. Of primary interest are the two objects—particularly the green mass and the red appendage; then the creased ground, followed by the background.

ALIGNMENT Each object occupies its own quadrant as defined by the folds of cloth. The left object leans over and rests on the right object precisely at the line ringing the top portion of the object. Both objects are aligned approximately parallel with the fabric fold line and the viewing plane.

SENSORIALITY The red appendage and the green object are vivid and evocative. The lower portions of both objects are full and smooth: broad with subtle, simple detailing. The top caps of both objects are more highly articulated and idiosyncratically shaped, particularly that of the left object. The ground beneath the objects is crisply folded—sharp ridges with pronounced shadows. The warm-gray background graduates from a darker shade at the bottom to lighter at the top. There is a generalized quality of "exaggerated presence" in every element of the arrangement.

METAPHOR The objects seem to be *containers for fluids* used in either the home or office: *different types* of the *same species*. The *whimsical* diminutive object has its *head resting* on the robust one's *broad shoulder*. The two objects seem like *friends or lovers*. The out-curving red appendage is an *affectionate or flirtatious gesture*. The gray background is like a *stormy sky*. The *rigorous grid* created by the fabric folds is like an *attenuated chess board*; each gridded space is like an *individualized place*.

MYSTIFICATION The enigma is, why is one object intentionally leaning on the other for support?

NARRATIVE There is an overall sense of drama and portentousness to the arrangement, but only one scenario—a small object leans on a larger object for support. There are, however, many possible sub- or supraplots. For example, the objects are child and parent, or lovers, or just good friends. Perhaps this is all a scene from an avant garde opera played out by objects; a gathering storm approaches and. . . .

COHERENCE The arrangement is sensorially engaging, very readable, and bound tightly together by a narrative, although an ambiguous one: obscurity and great coherence simultaneously.

RESONANCE The pervasive, mysterious sensuality of the arrangement is beguiling. A wide spectrum of imaginative possibilities is suggested by the seemingly theatrical anthropomorphism. There is a lot going on here to engage the imagination for quite a while.

Back cover

HIERARCHY The spiral configuration is the most striking visual element. Then the darker component objects become of interest, followed by the lighter ones.

ALIGNMENT All the objects are aligned into the precise shape of a spiral. The spacing between each object is relatively the same.

SENSORIALITY The spiral is a graceful, compelling, geometric expression. The individual objects have modest to significant sensory appeal. The objects fall into three or four categories of form, from the highly detailed and articulated to the smooth, roundish, somewhat nondescript. The overall arrangement color scheme is neutral, with a few black and bright pastels thrown in for a touch of piquancy. The background is a warm, neutral color.

METAPHOR The specific type of objects, together with the *sand-colored* background, is an allusion to *the seashore*. The spiral shape seems to serve *no functional purpose* other than a display of *decorative tinkering*.

NARRATIVE Someone picked up these objects along an ocean beach and innocently fashioned them into a spiral.

COHERENCE There is only one clear and consistent theme here: playful arranging at the seashore. There are absolutely no extraneous or distracting elements.

RESONANCE The spiral is an evocative shape, and the objects may evoke personal or tactile memories. On the other hand, there is a static, somewhat simplistic, quality to the overall composition. You are inclined to muse, but not too deeply or too long.

NOTES

1. The terms "illustration" and "painting" and "illustrator," "painter," and "artist" are used somewhat interchangeably in this discussion. More precisely defined, an illustrator is someone whom you retain to create pictorial images that accord precisely with your program—i.e., your ideas. A painter, on the other hand, is someone who has his or her own program. If you commission work from a painter, it will be filtered through the painter's highly personal conception of how the pictorialization should be realized. The illustrations in this book were executed by a painter. I never suggested how the objects in the paintings should be exactly arranged, or even what objects to use.

2. See page 17 for the beginning of a discussion about the differences between arrangements of things in the real world and in artworks.

3. Obviously I could have had the arrangements repre-

sented by photographs instead of paintings. There are, however, certain pedagogical benefits to slightly ambiguous visual information. If the paintings were too realistic and detailed, you, the reader, might be seduced by the fascinating intricacies of the objects themselves and lose sight of the relationship of the objects to each other—the way they are arranged—which is the focus of this book.

4. This book started out as an attempt to understand what made the arrangements I saw in a San Francisco store, Japonesque, so extraordinary. For years I visited Japonesque and enjoyed the unique arrangements of ceramic, rock, old wood, plant materials—plus other sundry and eclectic objects—and wondered what it was that gave them their imaginative vitality. Of course I asked the proprietor/arranger (Koichi Hara) how he did what he did. But after a few conversations it became obvious that he was either unable, or unwilling, to articulate his secrets. Conversations with other creators of extraordinary arranging ability (Gary Weiss of IXIA in San Francisco, Len Morgan and Angus Wilke of Cove Landing in New York, Lee Hollingworth of Story in London, and Andreas Geis of Blumenkraft in Vienna) were similarly stimulating but ultimately fruitless at getting to the explicable roots of great arrangement. I pragmatically concluded that there was no algorithm or formula for exceptional arrangement design, yet I suspected that the conceptual principles of superior arrangement must exist—or could be manufactured—and that I could find them if I just persisted. So I changed my methodology. Instead of relying on arrangement practitioners for insights, I attacked the literature of art, art history, criticism, merchandising display, communication theory, literary theory . . . until I chanced upon rhetoric (see page 24). Anyway, I had my rhetoric epiphany six months after I had commissioned the paintings.

5. To limit the scope of the subject matter, this book is primarily concerned with the *arranging*, not the selection, of objects. (Object selection should be the subject of another book.) Arrangement is defined as the intentional placement of objects, even if the arrangement seems acci-

dental or indifferent. It is always assumed, for the purposes of this book, that there is a human agent behind an arrangement's creation, either actively or passively.

6. At many of the larger retail chains—and most of the fashion-involved ones—prototypical arrangements are designed at central headquarters and transmitted by fax, e-mail, or courier service around the world to satellite stores. Alternatively, arranging specialists are flown to individual store locations to do the hands-on arrangement. At the very least, large retail organizations issue updated "style manuals" with directives indicating the elements and parameters of permissible arranging schemes. At the time I was researching this book in San Francisco, the Agnes B shop received weekly e-mails from Paris with drawings and measurements indicating the exact placement of objects in the window display. The Bottega Veneta shop received photographs every couple of weeks from New York headquarters indicating what objects to place exactly where. At the Versace boutique somebody comes from New York headquarters periodically to do the main displays; otherwise a local independent merchandise arranger is brought in to set up the arrangements in consultation with the New York people . . . . I also visited the main Armani complex of boutiques in Milan. Arranging of objects there is done according to a "manual of visual display design parameters."

7. "Communicating something" means transmitting meaning—any kind of meaning—to the arrangement's viewers, or, in a self-reflective way, back to the arranger her/himself.

8. Natural languages undoubtedly began as attempts to coordinate descriptions of, and references to, the physical world of objects and other kinds of things. But a developed language requires (a) a consistent and widely understood means of combining (syntax) and (b) a shared pool of common symbols (vocabulary). At the present time, the domain of arranging things generally has neither. In some subcultures, however, like the extended community of Japanese Tea Ceremony practitioners, there exists a com-

monly understood syntax and vocabulary of arranging things within the tearoom. But this is a very insular and narrow context, interesting but of little relevance to arranging in the wide-ranging everyday sense that this book is focusing on.

9. According to Charles Sterling, in his book *Still Life Painting: From Antiquity to the Present Time* (Paris: Editions Pierre Tisné, 1959), still life pictorial representations existed at least since the 3rd century B.C.E. Sterling gives the example of a humorous mosaic mural by Sosos of Pegamum entitled *The Unswept Room* "in which remnants of food—fish bones, chicken bones, claws of shellfish, half-eaten fruit, nutshells and pips—are seen scattered over the floor, as if the servants had neglected to sweep the triclinium after banquet."

10. "Meaning," a complex word, is used often in this book in the sense of "plausible inference"—a functional interpretation that can be used to deduce, confirm, predict, and infer other meanings. For example, when you see a foil-wrapped chocolate on your pillow upon returning to your hotel room in the evening, you may reasonably assume that it is yours to eat, or to keep. This kind of meaning is inculcated through our social/cultural systems. To the extent that other people understand the same meanings, we can communicate; these shared meanings create our common world, our common reality. Another aspect of meaning also implied in this book is meaning as affective sensations—feelings and emotions. Affective meanings tend to vary a little more from person to person than does the aforementioned meaning in the sense of plausible inference.

11. James Elkins, in his book *Why Are Our Pictures Puzzles? On the Modern Origins of Pictorial Complexity* (New York and London: Routledge, 1999), skillfully explores and explains how and why works of art created prior to the 20th century, which at the time of their execution had straightforward meanings to the viewers of the period, have taken on increasingly farfetched meanings in our era.

12. Paintings with the *Vanitas* themes, highlighting the folly and ephermerality of human life, were first executed in Holland but were subsequently painted throughout Europe. Viewers of these paintings probably didn't use terms like "allusion" and "metaphor" but just naturally made the interpretative connections because still life paintings up to this point in history had always had obvious, easy-to-discern symbolic meanings.

13. Using this painting as an example was purely arbitrary. Thousands of other artworks could have been used to exemplify this point. I was simply leafing through the pages of *Still Life: A History* (by Sybille Ebert-Schifferer, translated from the German by Russell Stockman, New York: Harry N. Abrams, Inc., Publishers, 1999) when I came upon an appealing reproduction of this image.

14. Not all art is "not arranging." That is, not all art uses nonstandard or obscure references—or tries to sabotage conventional meanings and readings. But, to emphasize the points here, I am focusing on the art that does.

15. Arrangements of things in the normal, everyday world sometimes look exactly the same as the arrangements of things that you might encounter in an art gallery or museum. Following are a few of the ways in which arrangements of things in the "real world" differ from arrangements of things in the "art world."

real world Arrangements have no titles.
art world Artworks always have titles. Even "Untitled" is a title designating a work of art.

real world You already possess all the information you need to understand an arrangement. Arrangements exist in the realm of everyday common sense and social knowledge.
art world You have to learn how to "read" artworks. Understanding art means specialized knowledge of the contemporary "art dialogue" plus the historical canons of style, theme, subject matter, symbolism, and meaning.

real world Arrangements have to interact with real things in the real, immediate environment.

art world Artworks are part of a self-contained conceptual system set apart from the real world.

real world An arrangement lives or dies solely on its own merits; what you see is what you get.
art world Artworks are buttressed by artist statements; museum/gallery press releases and advertisements; museum/gallery explanatory tours, tapes, and videos; art criticism. . . .

real world Things in arrangements never entirely lose their sense of tangible, physical reality.
art world Things in artworks can also be represented abstractly or conceptually; that is, non-materially.

16. Here, as elsewhere in this book, I am making an overly sweeping statement that ignores the exceptions for the sake of moving my argument along. I'm sure that there are arrangers who think deeply and analytically about their arranging process, although I have never met one. My contention is that such an intellectual faculty would, in most cases, be a worthwhile addition to the most intuitive of approaches. A case in point: While researching this book in Paris, I walked down an arty street of mostly antique and related shops, peering into the various window displays. Just inside a frame-maker's shop I noticed an elaborate arrangement of large rocks, picture frames, and walls painted bright blue. Curious, I stepped inside and asked the proprietor what the arrangement meant. "Absolutely nothing," he confidently replied. We chatted for a few minutes; I persisted, I prodded. Finally he suggested, "Well, maybe it has to do with the seashore, with the ocean. Come to think of it—yes, yes!— I've just come back from from a vacation on the coast, so maybe. . . ." Would a more self-aware, critical understanding of what he was doing have made his arrangement more effective? I think so.

17. This language is from *Visual Merchandising: The Business of Merchandise Presentation* by Robert Colborne (Albany, New York: Delmar, 1996).

18. One approach to arranging things that crossed my

mind was mix-and-match arranging templates: presenting archetypal arrangement motifs, formats, rules—whatever—in a reference-book format. In such an approach, a grab bag of arranging ideas are put together in a systematic form. I rejected this idea because I thought extraordinary arranging would more likely be approached in a more open-ended manner. Templates essentially create closed, constrained systems. (Yet in a sense, the rhetorical scheme outlined later in this book is a kind of template: a template for thinking.)

19. I subsequently discovered I wasn't the only person who had the idea of using rhetoric as a tool for exploring communicational phenomena. A number of interesting rhetorical approaches, primarily as applied to literature or the media (TV, advertising, and the like), are described in both *Rhetorical Criticism: Exploration and Practice*, 2nd edition, by Sonja K. Foss (Prospect Heights, Illinois: Waveland Press, Inc., 1996) and in *Modern Rhetorical Criticism*, 2nd edition, by Roderick P. Hart (Needham, Massachusetts: Allyn and Bacon, 1997).

20. From Book 1, Chapter 2 of Aristotle's *Rhetoric*, written circa 330 B.C.E., translated by W. Rhys Roberts. Although Aristotle was far from the first person to write about rhetoric, his work is the oldest complete extant text on the subject.

21. Persuasive ability is, of course, one of the principle skills needed for survival in human society.

22. While there is little dispute among historians about the basic outlines of rhetoric's history, there is some disagreement about the specific roles and influences of the agents of invention and transmission. Books I have enjoyed that offer provocative and plausible alternative theories include *Rereading the Sophists: Classical Rhetoric Refigured* by Susan C. Jarratt (Carbondale and Edwardsville: Southern Illinois University Press, 1991) and *The Beginnings of Rhetorical Theory in Classical Greece* by Edward Schiappa (New Haven and London: Yale University Press, 1999).

23. In addition to argumentative logic, the Sophists also taught linguistic devices like figures of speech, skillful delivery, and other oratory techniques useful for persuasion and influence over others. The Sophists developed an unsavory reputation due to, among other reasons, their philosophic relativism. Sophistic training included how to argue both sides of the same issue. Sophists embraced the notion of the pluralistic reality that is created by the contradiction of opposing points of view. The Sophists did not believe that persuading someone to agree with your point of view is the same thing as convincing them of the truth. In fact, the Sophists didn't believe in eternal and immutable truths; this got them in trouble because it was contrary to the prevailing intellectual fashion.

24. Rhetoric came into being in Greece at roughly the same heady historic moment as: (a) the conscious development of abstract thought, (b) the beginning of widespread literacy, (c) a shift away from mythic narrative in favor of rational analysis as a means of understanding natural phenomena, (d) a culture-wide agreement that the authority of law derived from man, not from divine sources, and (e) the development of democracy.

25. Once fully assembled as a standard body of knowledge between the 4th century B.C.E. and the end of antiquity, rhetoric has remained essentially the same down to the present. For more on the orthodox history of rhetoric see *A New History of Classical Rhetoric* by George A. Kennedy (Princeton: Princeton University Press, 1994).

26. For example, there is basically no such thing as a non-rhetorically-charged description of anything. Peace officer, officer of the law, policeman, cop, pig: five ways, in order of descending respect, of describing the same thing. All communication requires the use of terms that have intrinsic persuasive value, one way or another. As a consequence, the term "rhetoric" is sometimes disparagingly used today as a synonym for decorative, hyperbolic, manipulative, or propagandistic speech.

27. If I stray too far from the proven usefulness of the

2,500-year-old strain of classical rhetoric, I risk losing whatever inherent authority the tradition offers and my reconfigured rhetoric could degenerate into nothing more than personal conjecture. On the other hand, if I'm successful in my "radical" reconceptualization, it might suggest that rhetoric can be extended to all manner of visual things.

28. Filtering information through another medium yields a different way of looking at things. Like recipes manifested on the pages of a cookbook rather than on a plate, you see the food with new understanding.

29. The meaning of precision/precise alignment could be, depending on the specific arrangement context, "formality," "rationality," "neatness," "the presence of a controlling intelligence," "authoritarianism," and so on.

30. The principle of mystification is not present in every arrangement.

31. You should keep in mind that all of the following analyses/interpretations in this section are based *only* on the author's point-of-view. You, the reader, may have perfectly valid analyses/interpretations of the same arrangements that differ from those of the author. For example, where I may see/feel "rationality" in an arrangement, you may see/feel "psychological comfort," and so on. The point is not a "right" or "wrong" interpretation, but a *useful* interpretation, that is, analyses and interpretations that give more insight into the process of creating effective arrangements.

Something else to consider: the analyses presented in this book are truncated for editorial reasons (a very short book, for designers, just to give an indication of how it's done . . .). Needless to say, every arrangement presented here can be investigated at much greater length.

32. The "viewing plane" is the angle of view you, the viewer, have if you stand or sit in front of the arrangement.

33. For legibility, metaphors and other kinds of metaphoric process are italicized in this section of the book.

34. A "culture set" or "arrangement set" is an arrangement you see over and over again, so much so that it becomes/is a "root visual metaphor"—a cultural archetype used in other visual allusions and metaphors. Often culture sets/arrangement sets indicate, or prepare us for, an activity about to take place—like a table setting "inviting you" to a meal. Or a couch with plush throw pillows, arranged just so, "beckoning you" to sit down and relax.

About the author

Leonard Koren, who lives in San Francisco and Tokyo, trained as an artist and architect. He created and published *WET (The Magazine of Gourmet Bathing)*, one of the premier avant garde publications of the 1970s. Subsequently he has produced books, mainly about design and aesthetics. His recent works include *Wabi-Sabi: for Artists, Designers, Poets & Philosophers*, *Undesigning the Bath*, and *Gardens of Gravel and Sand.*

About the illustrator

Nathalie Du Pasquier was born in Bordeaux, France and since 1979 has lived in Milan, Italy. Until 1987 she worked as a designer. She was a founding member of Memphis, the design group, for which she made numerous textiles, objects, and furniture. Since 1987 she has dedicated herself mainly to painting, specifically "still life painting": arrangements of objects on the canvas.

Thanks

The following people helped, in great and small ways, in the making of this book: Christie Bartlett, the staff at Blumenkraft (Vienna), Alison Evans, Gay Gassmann, Andreas Geis, Koichi Hara, Lee Hollingworth, Sarah Hollywood, Salvatore Lacagnina, Esther Mitgang, Len Morgan, Sue Parker, Janet Pollock, Brigitte Prinzgau, Barbara Radice, Christof Radl, Ettore Sottsass, Meredith Tromble, Gary Weiss, Angus Wilke, and Jane Withers. For technical support I want to express my appreciation to Ilvio Gallo, Kina Sullivan, the management and staff of Plus Color (Milan), and especially Bill Tom for his expert typographic advice. Lastly, I want to express my gratitude to Peter Goodman, my wise editor; Nathalie Du Pasquier, my artistic collaborator; and Ziggie Kato, the one who keeps my life always interesting.